LOOKING FOR LEARNING

LOOSE PARTS

How to identify learning in child-initiated play

LAURA ENGLAND

FEATHERSTONE

FEATHERSTONE
Bloomsbury Publishing Plc
50 Bedford Square, London, WC1B 3DP, UK
29 Earlsfort Terrace, Dublin 2, Ireland

BLOOMSBURY, FEATHERSTONE and the Feather logo are trademarks of Bloomsbury Publishing Plc

First published in Great Britain 2019 by Bloomsbury Publishing Plc
Text copyright © Laura England, 2019
Photographs © Laura England, Shutterstock, 2019

Laura England has asserted her right under the Copyright, Designs and Patents Act, 1988,
to be identified as Authors of this work

A catalogue record for this book is available from the British Library

ISBN: PB: 978-1-4729-6301-7; ePDF: 978-1-4729-6300-0; ePub: 978-1-4729-6299-7

4 6 8 10 9 7 5 3

Series design: Lynda Murray

Printed and bound in India by Replika Press Pvt. Ltd.

MIX
Paper from
responsible sources
FSC® C016779

To find out more about our authors and books visit www.bloomsbury.com and sign up for our newsletters

Contents

Introduction

Loose parts have been a fundamental part of my practice for many years. Without even knowing it, and long before I even entered the world of teaching, I enjoyed exploring loose parts. Although the concept of loose parts is nothing new, as practitioners we need to understand the learning that takes place during loose parts play. This book will take you on a journey, delving deep into my practice and the thoughts and actions of the small people I have had the pleasure of working with on a daily basis, without whom this book would have never come to fruition.

I strongly believe that it's the deep understanding and the connections we make with young children that allow us to understand the learning that's taking place, which is why throughout this book you will gain an insight into some of the loose parts play I have observed and how this shaped my thoughts and ideas.

We will start by looking at what loose parts are and some of the theories that underpin them and loose parts play. We will then look at the benefits of loose parts play before moving on to look at how it links to the statutory framework for the early years foundation stage (2017) through the connections between loose parts and the characteristics of effective learning and also the seven areas of learning. Finally, you will find some practical advice on sourcing loose parts and how to introduce them.

WHAT ARE LOOSE PARTS?

Loose parts come in many different shapes and sizes; they're objects with no predetermined purpose that can be used in a variety of ways. Lisa Daly and Miriam Beloglovsky (2015) describe loose parts in their book, *Loose Parts: Inspiring Play in Young Children*, as materials that:

> *Children can carry, combine, redesign, line up, take apart and put... back together in almost endless ways.*

When it comes to loose parts, it's less about the materials you provide and more about allowing resources to be used in unique ways, giving children the opportunity to discover, create, explore, experiment and invent freely. As I said previously, it's nothing new. You only need to look back at your own childhood and the hours spent combining petals and water to create 'perfume', or when children used sticks as swords and created patterns in mud, sand and snow. Boredom and lack of technological distractions led us, as children, to be creative with freely-available resources. This boredom is less prevalent with the meteoric rise in technology and although technology has its place, even in loose parts play, we are in danger of raising a generation of children that are less creative, inventive or inquisitive. Because of this, loose parts play has seen a resurgence as more and more practitioners see its potential for the all-round development of children in the early years and beyond.

The theory of loose parts play

THE ORIGINS OF LOOSE PARTS PLAY

The term 'loose parts' was first introduced by architect Simon Nicholson in the 1970s in his paper 'The Theory of Loose Parts'. Nicholson believes that everyone has the ability to be creative, and it's the restrictions put on play that reduce creativity for young children. Even now, we can see that overly-planned and structured environments take away the child's need to be creative and think critically and, as mentioned earlier, the rise in technology means that children don't need to be creative as they're constantly stimulated by the availability of computers, tablets, mobile phones and games consoles.

Nicholson (1972) described loose parts as variables and provided examples of these variables:

> There is evidence that all children love to interact with variables, such as materials and shapes; smells and other physical phenomena, such as electricity, magnetism and gravity; media such as gases and fluids; sounds, music, motion; chemical interactions, cooking and fire; and other humans, and animals, plants, words, concepts and ideas. With all these things all children love to play, experiment, discover and invent and have fun. All these things have one thing in common, which are variables or 'loose parts'.

Nicholson goes on to say:

> In any environment, both the degree of inventiveness and creativity, and the possibility of discovery, are directly proportional to the number and kind of variables in it.

Put simply, the more open-ended resources that we provide for young children, the more creativity we will see. This is supported by the theory of affordance.

THE THEORY OF AFFORDANCE

James J. Gibson (1979) introduced us to the theory of affordance. He believed that environments and objects are viewed differently depending on the individual; the 'affordances' of an environment or object are based on the potential that it has. He defined affordances in terms of the environment and animals:

> The affordances of the environment are what it offers the animal, what it provides or furnishes, either for good or ill. The verb to afford is found in the dictionary, but the noun affordance is not. I have made it up. I mean by it something that refers to both the environment and the animal in a way that no existing term does. It implies the complementarity of the animal and the environment.

When applied to children, Theresa Casey and Juliet Robertson (2016) share a great example of what the affordances of a wall have to offer:

> ... a brick wall may be built to make a clear boundary between a pavement and a garden but for many children, it would offer a place to sit, walk along, balance, hide behind and jump off.

The above definition gives us a clear sense of how environments made up of loose parts and open-ended resources can be many different things to the many different children that encounter them. These environments offer endless opportunities only limited by the views and perceptions of the child. This is closely linked to schema theory, as well as the philosophy of the Reggio Emilia approach.

SCHEMA THEORY

A schema, often referred to as a 'pattern of play', is used to describe the repetitive behaviours of young children. The word 'schema' was first introduced by Jean Piaget (1952), and he defined it as:

> *... a cohesive, repeatable action sequence possessing component actions that are tightly interconnected and governed by a core meaning.*

Put simply, schemas are patterns of behaviour that allow young children to construct knowledge and understanding of how the world works. For example, you may notice a child consistently dropping items from a high chair or persistently throwing things across a room. Both are signs of schema exploration as young children make sense of how items work and how their bodies affect change. There are lots of different identifiable schemas, but the most common schemas include:

CONNECTING: An interest in connecting things together. A child exploring this schema may be fascinated by doors or sticky tape. They may enjoy creating junk models using scrap materials.

TRAJECTORY: An interest in lines which may be shown through a child's need to run up and down, drop items from a height and throw objects.

ROTATION: An interest in items that roll and circular items. This may be shown through a child's interest in wheels, balls and rolling their bodies.

ENCLOSING: An interest in creating enclosures around objects or themselves. This may be seen when a child creates enclosures with blocks or cushions or places loose parts within items such as bangles.

ENVELOPING: An interest in hiding or covering objects and themselves. Children exploring this schema may repeatedly cover themselves with blankets.

TRANSFORMING: An interest in combining and changing materials. This may be shown through an interest in mixing water and sand together.

POSITIONING: An interest in sorting and placing items specifically. Children exploring this schema may enjoy tidying items into their rightful place.

ORIENTATION: An interest in viewing the world differently. Children exploring this schema may enjoying swinging and looking through their legs.

TRANSPORTING: An interest in moving objects or themselves from one place to another. This may be evident by children filling up bags to transport items from one place to another or by transporting water from one container to another.

Again, schema theory has strong links to children being able to freely explore and to use materials in lots of different ways depending on their line of enquiry. Therefore, children will use the environment in terms of its 'affordance' to them as an individual. Loose parts and open-ended materials will provide children with lots of opportunities to extend their learning through whichever schema they're exploring because they will use materials in different ways. For example, a child exploring a trajectory schema may line sticks up from one end of the room to the other, whereas a child exploring an enclosing schema may use the sticks to create enclosures around farm animals during small world play.

THE REGGIO EMILIA APPROACH

Reggio Emilia is a place in Italy, renowned for its approach to the teaching and learning of children in the early years. The Reggio Emilia approach, named after its place of origin, was established by Loris Malaguzzi just after World War Two when women whose husbands had died in the war called for help to look after their children.

Malaguzzi worked alongside the children with help from many of the families involved. As more of the Reggio schools opened, the fundamental principles they followed were established and include:

- Children are capable of constructing their own learning and should have control over the direction that it takes

- Children must be able to learn through all of their senses

- Children are natural communicators and should be given opportunities to form relationships with other children

- Adults are mentors and partners in learning.

The benefits of using loose parts

Loose parts offer a multitude of benefits for children of all ages. For children in the early years, here are some of the reasons why loose parts and loose parts play are highly regarded as an essential part of children's learning.

Creating a love for learning

We live in a society where the landscape of the job market is forever changing, particularly with continuing advances in technology. This means that it's more important than ever that we foster a love for learning from the earliest stages and that we continue to foster this love throughout childhood and beyond. When we talk about a love for learning we are talking about the child's ability to problem solve, explore, think critically and to try again. This will build resilient learners; learners who aren't afraid of failure and learners who want to continue to learn throughout their lives.

Loose parts play fosters this love for learning because it allows children to follow their own learning journey. Because there is no predetermined outcome young children can follow their own interests and try out different activities without being restricted by a right or wrong way to use resources.

Harnessing creativity

Again, when we look at the changing landscape of the job market, lots of manual jobs can be completed by robots. This means that the ability to be creative is an extremely important skill for future job prospects. Loose parts play naturally allows for creativity because there is no objective or outcome; children are free to follow any direction they want and to understand that there are endless possibilities.

Impacting on positive wellbeing

We are currently facing a rise in mental health issues, especially in children and teenagers, which is down to, in part, a fear of failure and an inability to deal with problems in an effective way. Loose parts with their endless possibilities and solutions remove this fear and instead promote problem solving and critical thinking.

> When children interact with loose parts they enter a world of 'what if' that promotes the type of thinking that leads to problem-solving and theoretical reasoning. Loose parts enhance children's ability to think imaginatively and see solutions, and they bring a sense of adventure and excitement to children's play.
>
> Daly and Beloglovsky (2015)

Establishing high levels of engagement

When children lead their own learning and can follow their own lines of enquiry they will have high levels of engagement. This is because what they're doing interests them and is relevant to their thoughts and ideas. As adults, we know that we are less interested in something we have been asked to do rather than something we have freely chosen to do ourselves. Take continuous professional development as an example. If you're reading this book because your manager or headteacher has told you to read it then you won't be as enthusiastic about it as someone who has picked it up out of the pure enjoyment of learning more about loose parts.

The reason high levels of engagement are so important is because high levels of engagement go hand in hand with high levels of learning. For the same reasons as above, it's because the learning is relevant to the child and their enquiries.

Lower levels of negative behaviour

The combination of all of the above: that love for learning, the impact on wellbeing and the higher levels of engagement lead to lower levels of negative behaviour. This is because there are less constraints on children's play.

Take story time for example. When we make children sit on the carpet to listen to a story that has most probably been chosen by one out of the 30 children, half of the children are already disinterested. Then consider the ten to 15 children that struggle to sit still because they aren't physically ready. Now think about how much time you spend reading the story to the remaining children who are engaged versus the time you spend telling the other children to sit still, to be quiet, to stop licking their hand and so on. In comparison, what you could do is spend 15 minutes enjoying the story with the handful of children that are engaged whilst the other children engage in something that interests them. Therefore, all children are learning and engaging at the same time.

Something that many practitioners worry about when using loose parts is the risks that may be associated with them. Firstly, there is a misconception surrounding loose parts that they're all items children can choke on. It's time to forget what we typically see loose parts as being and instead keep at the forefront of our minds that they're resources which are open-ended, resources which can be used in many different ways and resources that many settings already have. They're not just buttons, glass beads and nuts and bolts but they're blocks, lengths of fabric, leaves and sand. You can choose the level of risk you and your setting are comfortable with based on the ages and stages of the children you cater for. Every setting is unique as is every child which is why, throughout this chapter, I will provide ideas on how to introduce varying levels of loose parts play.

TINKER TRAYS

Tinker trays are a great way to introduce smaller parts to your preschool children in a safe and contained way. Put simply, a tinker tray is a small amount of lots of different items that children can explore and, as the name suggests, 'tinker' with. This is one of the very first ways that I introduce loose parts play in my setting. It very much starts out as adult-supervised experiences for the preschool-aged children (three- to four-year-olds).

A tinker tray is no riskier than providing children with art materials such as pom-poms, sequins, pipe cleaners and other small craft materials that we often use on a daily basis. However, the difference is that tinker trays give children freedom and control. There is no outcome with tinker trays, and therefore there are limited rules as to what children can do with the items. This is the part that most early years practitioners are cautious about but let me reassure you that children are far more capable at exploring, dissecting, discovering and experimenting when they have freedom. As discussed previously, when children are given control they're far less likely to use the materials in ways that we don't want them to.

Tinker tray idea

What you need:

- A tinker tray – this can be anything with compartments such as a cutlery or cupcake tray

- Small loose parts: beads, buttons, nuts and bolts, matchsticks, pebbles, corks, pom-poms, etc.

- Malleable materials: clay, play dough, salt dough, mud, etc.

What to do:

When you first introduce a tinker tray to the children in your setting, especially children who aren't used to having this much freedom, a great starting point is the addition of a malleable material. Give each child a good handful of your chosen malleable material and simply allow them to use it with the items in the tinker tray.

You can play alongside the children, modelling different ways that they might use the materials together. This may be by pushing items into the material, making prints with the items, covering the items and so on. As the children become more confident you will notice them combining the materials in ways you would never even imagine.

Another reason tinker trays are a really useful resource for practitioners is because they allow us to introduce new ideas and topics without it being forced upon the children. Instead, tinker trays allow us to give children the control and freedom to decide whether to engage with the materials and the new topic or not. Think about filling a tinker tray with seasonal items or items that represent seasonal holidays and celebrations.

Spring

- Flower buds
- Petals
- Straw
- Fake eggs
- Grass cuttings
- Bulbs

Summer

- Herb cuttings
- Shells
- Pebbles
- Drift wood pieces
- Sand
- Yellow pom-poms

Autumn

- Leaves
- Conkers
- Acorns
- Twigs
- Pine cones
- Orange pom-poms

Winter

- White pom-poms
- Silver sequins
- Small baubles
- Tinsel cuttings

As you can see from this list and the checklists in the next chapter, there are a huge range of loose parts to suit differing ages and stages, with varying levels of risk to ensure that even the most risk-sensitive settings can offer some form of loose parts play.

INVITATIONS

The concept behind tinker trays (giving children freedom and control to explore) is the same as providing an invitation or provocation for the children to explore. Although, as the practitioner, you're in control of the materials provided, which may or may not have a desired use, the children still have the freedom and choice to decide if they want to engage with the items or not. If a child does choose to engage with the invitation or provocation they have the freedom and choice as to how they want to engage with it.

An invitation or provocation invites or provokes a child to engage. This will often be a collection of items that ignite curiosity, awe and wonder which will entice the children to explore and play. You could add other resources to extend what the children do with the loose parts which might include weighing scales, magnifying glasses, scissors, etc.

Another invitation that you can change regularly, particularly good for pack-away settings or smaller settings, is a box or case of items that inspire children to be curious. Vintage suitcases filled with authentic or curious resources have become a popular addition to many settings. However, you don't need anything fancy if you want to introduce this on a low budget. A suitcase can be easily substituted with a large bag or box and you can use already existing resources to fill it, creating awe and wonder as the children explore the resources you already have in a new way.

Invitations in action

The invitation: We set up a block area with lots of different types of materials including wooden blocks, cardboard tubes and wooden slices.

Observation: We started to notice a pattern in the way in which the children accessed the blocks, many of them built towers and discussed whose was bigger.

Extension: We added measuring tubes to the area to encourage the children to continue to explore length and height.

Curious about metallics

What you need:

- A box, bag or suitcase
- Silver tinsel
- Plastic mirrors
- Metallic blocks
- Tins
- Metal utensils
- Silver sequins

What to do:

- For younger children, you can explore the contents of the box, allowing the children to handle the items and explore them on a sensory level.

- Allow children to combine the items, line them up, fill the tins with the tinsel and explore all those schematic behaviours.

- For older children, simply include the box in your continuous provision. You may add it in a particular area to enhance it, e.g. within the construction area to see how the children combine the materials with the blocks you already have.

INTRODUCING LOOSE PARTS TO BABIES

In addition to the risk, many practitioners also worry about the mess they think loose parts will create which is why it's important to introduce loose parts at the earliest possible stage. And yes, this does include babies! Introducing loose parts isn't a race. It takes time for other members of your team to get on board and for children to understand that loose parts play is going to be accessible all of the time. Start out slowly with fewer loose parts and build this up over time. An example that many practitioners can relate to is water play. When we get water play out once a week for children to explore, every single child will flock to it, splashing and getting excited. Whereas, when water play is an everyday occurrence within the setting, children understand that there is no rush to use it and that it will be there the following day. This leads to much more purposeful play. The water play example can be applied to loose parts. Every time we introduce a new loose part, the children are excited and curious to explore it which is why we should introduce loose parts in smaller quantities rather than all at once.

There is also no need to shudder at the thought of loose parts in the baby room. We need to remember that loose parts are nothing new – block play and treasure baskets are a staple for every baby room and offer the same benefits and experiences as smaller or riskier loose parts. They're open-ended, developmentally appropriate and foster creativity and critical thinking. Here is a list of loose parts suitable for babies:

Loose parts for babies

Blocks

Blocks come in many different shapes, sizes and materials. Even on their own, they can create an engaging and inviting loose parts play resource for babies. I also believe that good blocks are worth investing in. They will last a lifetime if cared for properly and can be used by all ages and stages of development. We often rotate our blocks throughout the setting. Be on the lookout for different types of blocks: metallic, clear, light up and in varying shapes. You can add plastic cable reels, tin cans (you can buy safety tin openers that leave a smooth edge) and large log slices alongside your blocks for further investigation and exploration.

Cardboard

Another great resource that's open-ended but safe is cardboard. You can collect cardboard boxes, tubes, egg cartons and rolls by reusing all the packaging and waste from your kitchen. And, as it's easily replenished, it doesn't matter if it gets ruined.

Treasures

Lots of standard treasure basket items are great loose parts: brushes, wooden items, wicker balls, fabric and curtain hoops are all safe and large enough for babies to handle. From the very youngest babies who will explore the items through their senses, right up to two-year-olds who will explore using schemas, treasure baskets are a great resource.

Sensory

Our sensory room is filled with loose parts: light up blocks, pebbles and rollers which are all great for stacking, rolling and exploring. In addition to these, provide lots of lengths of fabrics including tulle, cotton, hessian and sequin.

Outdoors

Outdoors is a great place to introduce loose parts play. Firstly, there are a wealth of natural loose parts in many outdoor environments that most children will already be acquainted with, therefore, making it the perfect place for practitioners to observe play and gain a deeper understanding of how children are already using the loose parts around them.

Secondly, there is a lot more space outdoors for children to use larger loose parts and engage in risky play. Risky play is extremely important because it doesn't only encompass each area of learning, but it brings the characteristics of effective learning to the forefront. Building confident, willing, independent and creative learners is what the ethos of loose parts play is all about. As previously discussed, we cannot begin to imagine the type of subject knowledge children will need to engage with in the future, but we can ensure that children have the right attitude and mental wellbeing to cope. Risk taking appeals to nearly all children but it particularly engages those children that find it difficult to sit still and listen for long periods of time (something which cannot be expected of many young children) and, as practitioners, we should embrace this style of learning and exploit it to our advantage.

Risk is most relevant to children when they're playing with and exploring larger loose parts, therefore this is the best time to talk to them about managing risks for themselves. When children are playing with large loose parts such as cable reels, crates and wooden planks they often build structures which require lifting and balancing cumbersome objects. Talking to the children about how the objects should be carried, perhaps suggesting different numbers of people dependent on the weight and size, will minimise associated risks. Talking through with the children that they need to let go of a positioned object slowly to ensure it will stay in place also minimises associated risks. However, always be aware that as a facilitator you want the children to use their own knowledge, so don't give them the answers but make comments such as, 'That looks too heavy for one person' and 'I don't know if that's small enough to fit on top', which will trigger them to think about it too.

Sourcing loose parts

Sourcing loose parts isn't difficult, but it does take time as you will need to add to your collection over the years as you collect interesting items from a range of different sources. Be sure to check out local charity shops and car boot sales where you can pick up wooden and wicker items fairly cheaply. What is desirable to early years practitioners is often seen as outdated by sellers and this is where there are bargains to be had. You can also ask local businesses if they have any scrap materials that may be useful: garages will give you scrap tyres for free and electrical suppliers will have cable reels aplenty. One of your best sources for acquiring loose parts are parents. We have had giant bolts donated from a parent who worked on the railway lines and barriers from a parent who is a builder.

If you're unsure about what to collect then loose parts can be split into a number of categories. You will want to look out for items made of a variety of materials including plastic items, natural materials, metal objects, fabric supplies, wooden items, paper goods, glass objects and ceramic items. Loose parts can vary hugely depending on where you live and what you have access to. It would be near impossible to create an exhaustive list of loose parts to collect but here are some ideas if you're starting out.

Plastic

- Bottle tops
- PVC pipes
- Guttering
- Reels
- Tubs
- Curtain rings
- Old board game pieces
- Straws
- Hula hoops
- Bottles
- Beads
- Cups
- Tyres
- Bubble wrap
- Balls
- Funnels
- Buttons

Natural

- Sticks
- Stones
- Conkers
- Twigs
- Rocks
- Flowers
- Gravel
- Snow
- Logs
- Pebbles
- Vegetables
- Moss
- Feathers
- Pods
- Leaves
- Seeds
- Pine cones
- Shells
- Sand
- Acorns
- Water
- Clay
- Mud
- Dried fruit

Metal

- Spoons
- Jar lids
- Bike wheels
- Discs
- Keys
- Magnets
- Cutters
- Tin foil
- Springs
- Nuts and bolts
- Washers
- Curtain rings
- Bangles
- Chains
- Tin cans

Fabric

- Doilies
- Lace
- Rope
- Hessian sacks
- String
- Bobbles
- Felt
- Thread
- Wool
- Carpet tiles
- Pom-poms
- Burlap
- Scarves
- Silk
- Chiffon
- Leather
- Twine
- Ribbon

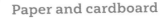

Paper and cardboard

- Shoe boxes
- Egg boxes
- Cartons
- Tubes
- Paper cups
- Paper plates
- Shredded paper
- Wrapping paper
- Masking tape
- Stickers

Wooden

- Wooden pegs
- Napkin rings
- Bangles
- Spools
- Decking planks
- Cable reels
- Dowels
- Chair legs
- Wooden beads

Glass and Ceramics

- Marbles
- Mirrors
- Sea glass
- Glass beads
- Tiles
- Flower pots
- Slate
- Gems
- Reels
- Beads
- Crystals

The characteristics of effective learning

When looking at the resources and activities we provide for children on a daily basis we must consider the differing styles of learning that young children have. Some children enjoy learning through particular interests, others enjoy tinkering or experimenting, and some enjoy completing a task or achieving an outcome. Whatever style of learning, an environment filled with lots of loose parts will enable children to interact with resources differently. For example, children who enjoy the end product of what they're doing may enjoy sorting pencils in colour order whereas children who enjoy problem solving might enjoy testing how different materials can be combined. An environment filled with loose parts and flexible practitioners will benefit every style of learning.

PLAYING AND EXPLORING	ACTIVE LEARNING	CREATING AND THINKING CRITICALLY
Finding out and exploring	**Being involved and concentrating**	**Having their own ideas**
• Showing curiosity about objects, events and people • Using senses to explore the world around them • Engaging in open-ended activity • Showing particular interests	• Maintaining focus on their activity for a period of time • Showing high levels of energy, fascination • Not easily distracted • Paying attention to details	• Thinking of ideas • Finding ways to solve problems • Finding new ways to do things
Playing with what they know	**Keeping on trying**	**Making links**
• Pretending objects are things from their experience • Representing their experiences in play • Taking on a role in their play • Acting out experiences with other people	• Persisting with activity when challenges occur • Showing a belief that more effort or a different approach will pay off • Bouncing back after difficulties	• Making links and noticing patterns in their experience • Making predictions • Testing their ideas • Developing ideas of grouping, sequences, cause and effect
Being willing to 'have a go'	**Enjoying achieving what they set out to do**	**Choosing ways to do things**
• Initiating activities • Seeking challenge • Showing a 'can do' attitude • Taking a risk, engaging in new experiences, and learning by trial and error	• Showing satisfaction in meeting their own goals • Being proud of how they accomplished something – not just the end result • Enjoying meeting challenges for their own sake rather than external rewards or praise	• Planning, making decisions about how to approach a task, solve a problem and reach a goal • Checking how well their activities are going • Changing strategy as needed • Reviewing how well the approach worked

Development Matters in the Early Years Foundation Stage (2012)

So far, this book has looked at what loose parts are, their benefits and their role in promoting the characteristics of effective learning. Throughout this next section we will look at each area of learning, as outlined by the statutory framework for the early years foundation stage (2017), and the role that loose parts play in promoting children's development within the early years. Each area of learning follows a similar pattern to enable you to dip in and out as necessary. Each chapter starts with an introduction to the area of learning and includes 'looking for learning' observations of loose parts play in action, enabling you to understand how it links to areas of development. You will also find lots of ideas for extending loose parts play to encourage development in the area as well as extension resource ideas.

Personal, social and emotional development

Personal, social and emotional development is split into three aspects which include: making relationships, self-confidence and self-awareness, and managing feelings and behaviour. I find, and have found myself also doing this in the past, that many practitioners develop these aspects through abstract teaching whereby, for example, we talk about emotions through the use of puppets and books rather than through real-life interactions. I only need to spend 30 minutes with a cohort of children and within that time I will witness varying emotions from anger to happiness, sadness to confusion. Instead of planning times to teach the children about emotions, I teach children about them when they're real and relevant. You're probably wondering where loose parts and loose parts play fit into this and we will look at each aspect in turn.

MAKING RELATIONSHIPS

For younger children, making relationships is about sharing experiences and exploring new situations with a familiar adult. Moving forward, children will become more confident to explore situations on their own and to build relationships with other children through play, whereby they will initiate conversations, respond to the play of others and demonstrate friendly behaviour. We can link loose parts to making relationships by providing lots of new resources for younger children to explore alongside a familiar adult. Loose parts give children the freedom to initiate play, form special relationships with children who have similar interests and to be creative. This loose parts play allows children to explain their understanding and to question others. Here is an of example, from my own practice, of loose parts play in action where children are developing the 'making relationships' strand of their personal, social and emotional development.

LOOKING FOR LEARNING:
EXPLORING TREASURE BASKETS

Treasure baskets have been a key resource for every early years practitioner and essentially, they're a basket full of loose parts.

Observation: I sat on the floor and began to look through a treasure basket filled with autumnal objects: leaves, a small pumpkin, various coloured squashes and some pine cones. Some of the babies noticed the basket and crawled towards me, looking at the contents. One of the babies picked out a pine cone and put her finger between the pines. She thrust the pine cone towards me to gain my attention and when I acknowledged it she put her finger back between the pines. I put my hand out and she gave me the pine cone. She watched me as I rolled it on the back of my hand before I returned it to her.

What are the children learning? Through this observation we can see that the child is happy to explore the new resources alongside a familiar adult, seeking to gain the attention of the adult and allowing them to interact with the pine cone also.

The previous observation is an example of how children make relationships through simple interactions with adults. There is no need to plan in-depth sessions for this type of development. Instead, focus on sharing interactions and experiences via open-ended resources. As children develop their skills, you will notice that loose parts provide a wealth of opportunities for them to be creative which incorporates many other aspects of the making relationships strand.

Creativity can often allow children to work as a team and to discuss how and why they should do something, in addition to building skills such as listening to and understanding the views of others.

LOOKING FOR LEARNING:
LARGE LOOSE PARTS PLAY

Large loose parts such as tyres, planks of wood and cable reels usually invite children to work in teams to create things like an obstacle course, den or wherever else their imaginations lead them. This provides the perfect opportunity for children to develop the making relationships aspect of personal, social and emotional development.

Observation: A three-year-old boy climbed onto a cable reel and looked around at the other resources around him. These included tyres, decking planks, another cable reel and some crates. He jumped down from the cable reel and began to drag a decking plank towards the cable reel. He propped this up onto the cable reel and tried to pull a tyre towards the other end. He struggled to do this and looked to me for help. He asked me to move the tyre and I suggested that he ask a friend to help. He looked around and asked another child. Both children continued to move different resources to create an obstacle course. Throughout, they talked about which pieces should go where and why.

What are the children learning? As an adult, it would have been very easy for me to help the child to create his obstacle course, allowing him to tell me where he wants the pieces put. However, by introducing another child to the play he was building a relationship with the other child and developing vital skills such as understanding and explaining his viewpoint.

SELF-CONFIDENCE AND SELF-AWARENESS

This aspect of personal, social and emotional development is very similar for younger children to what has already been discussed in relation to making relationships. It's all about building confidence through meaningful interactions and as children get older it's about them expressing preferences and interests, confidently selecting resources and interacting with other children during play. Loose parts play and the ethos behind it has a vital role in developing this confidence, by providing an environment that nurtures choice and independence. When we provide children with resources and an environment that removes predetermined outcomes and the idea of failure, we give them the confidence to thrive and to try new things.

REMOVING AREAS

One type of early years practice that I find to be limiting, not just for the children but for the adults in a setting, is the concept of areas. For example, many settings have a maths area filled with numbers, counting materials and parts for sorting. Although all these resources and opportunities are great, sometimes it narrows our perception of what maths is and labels children who don't engage with this area as having no interest in maths. In fact, these children may be learning all about shape, space and measure when building dens or learning all about numbers when counting blocks to see whose tower is bigger.

Other children may be unwilling to access a certain area due to a fear of failure – a quantity matching activity may feel daunting to a child, especially if they don't have the skills to quantity match correctly. The end result might be pushing the children who need the support further away from it and enticing only the children who already quantity match confidently. By disbanding these areas, as skilled practitioners, we can implement maths into all types of play, giving the children the confidence to explore concepts that are new and exciting to them.

Not having specific areas and thereby removing a fear of failure is just one way we can give children more confidence. Another way we can give children confidence is by making flexibility a priority. Adults should be flexible in their views towards children's learning and development. The environment should be flexible to reflect the differing cohorts that access it and the resources should be flexible – a toy telephone is a telephone but a box can be a castle, a car, a hiding space and much, much more.

It's really important that the whole team values loose parts play and its ethos. Rules should be firmly in place and understood by all adults. If children are allowed to mix the sand and water one day but are reprimanded for this behaviour the next (due to differing staff views) they will lose confidence and stop interacting with the environment in their unique ways.

MANAGING FEELINGS AND BEHAVIOUR

An aspect of development that we will all be very aware of is giving children the skills to manage their own feelings and behaviour. This is all about young children learning to express their feelings, responding to the feelings of others and learning to cooperate within boundaries. Through loose parts play, we can give children opportunities to develop their turn-taking skills, to understand how their actions affect others and to learn about boundaries in a positive way.

How to manage feelings and behaviour isn't always taught effectively through relevant contexts. Instead, children are expected to learn about them in an abstract way. Quite often children will develop their understanding of feelings and emotions when given opportunities to express themselves and by seeing other children talk about their feelings too. Making learning relevant to each child is extremely important. I have personal experience of this because my practice changed to include loose parts play due to issues surrounding behaviour.

If we cast our minds back to the 'large loose parts' observation (page 24), this is a prime example of play that requires teamwork and will often involve children needing to manage their feelings and behaviour in order to complete the task at hand. If they don't manage their feelings and behaviour, they risk ruining the play for themselves as they rely on the other child for support when lifting and moving items. Here is an example of children developing their skills when it's relevant to them and their play, as opposed to through abstract teaching.

Observation: As the boys continued to build their obstacle course, they disagreed on where they wanted to place the next tyre. Child A pulled the tyre towards him in an attempt to assert his authority. Child B pulled back which caused Child A to fall forward. Child A then pushed Child B, at which point I intervened. I was able to discuss with both children how they were feeling, explaining that it's okay to feel angry or sad, but it isn't okay to hurt each other. We discussed how they could solve the problem and, in the end, agreed that they would have two tyres instead of one. Both children apologised to each other and were happy to continue playing.

What are the children learning? Had I been leading this activity with a group of children, telling them where to place the items and explaining who was doing what, they wouldn't have had the opportunity to disagree and to discuss these feelings in the way that they were able to do here.

Another reason why loose parts play is integral to developing skills surrounding managing feelings and behaviour is because we can implement rules and boundaries in a positive way. The risks posed by loose parts lend themselves really well to discussions around safety. Putting the emphasis on rules and boundaries in relation to safety rather than behaviour will have a positive impact on both the children and the staff within the setting. I believe that most negative behaviour we witness is down to something not being right in the environment rather than a child being 'naughty'. A good example of this is when children are expected to sit for long periods of time. Those children who struggle with this are often labelled as 'naughty' but more often than not these children aren't actually ready to sit still for long periods and are dealing with some very strong impulses telling them to move. If we take away the pressure to sit still for extended periods of time, we take away that label as it ceases to be an issue.

Again, by looking at large loose parts play and providing a space for children to lift, climb, jump and swing we eradicate the need for children to climb onto chairs and jump off tables the minute the adult's back is turned. If something is becoming a problem, you need to find an alternative. In my setting we were finding that it wasn't safe for children to carry decking planks on their own. Instead of stopping this, we made a rule that two people always have to carry them, one at either end. Now, if a child is carrying a decking plank on their own we remind them that it's unsafe, and that they should ask a friend or adult for help. But remember, consistency is key, and all members of the team need to understand the rules and boundaries. Most importantly, practitioners need to understand why the rule is there so that it can be explained to the children properly.

Conclusion

When looking at loose parts play in relation to personal, social and emotional development we can see that it's very much its ethos that has the starring role. It isn't so much what the children decide to do with the loose parts but instead it's about giving them the choice, the freedom and the flexibility to gain confidence, to experience different emotions and to build relationships.

Communication and language

Communication and language is split into three aspects: listening and attention, understanding, and speaking. As with personal, social and emotional development it's the ethos of loose parts play that's important for this area of learning and development for young children, as they build the confidence to interact with resources, other children and adults.

LISTENING AND ATTENTION

Listening and attention is about children reacting to voices, having a natural instinct to explore and having the ability to concentrate on objects of their choosing. Moving forward, children will listen to music and stories and follow directions as they strengthen these skills.

Environments that put an emphasis on loose parts and open-ended play will flow freely and provide children with lots of freedom to learn. This will allow children to develop their listening and attention in ways that are relevant and meaningful to them as they engage in interactions that interest them. Just like adults, children will not be interested in every topic and every conversation. By allowing them to lead their own learning children will engage in listening skills in more than a superficial way – just because a child is sitting still on the carpet whilst you talk about the weather doesn't mean that they're listening to you! However, when a child wants to engage with the different resources you have provided, they're much more likely to listen to the rules or advice given to them as it has a direct benefit for them and their play. Furthermore, children are curious about loose parts because they have a wealth of textures, colours, scents and uses, giving children even more of a reason to listen and pay attention during their exploration.

Schema treasure baskets

Providing babies and young children with loose parts in the form of treasure baskets that engage their schematic impulses will develop their listening and attention skills. As children engage in schema play, watching and listening to adults, they will focus their attention in order to make sense of the world and how things work. Try providing the following treasure baskets in your continuous provision.

Connection treasure basket: Fill a basket with hairbands, scrunchies, lengths of fabric, laces, zips, magnets and bangles so that children can explore how items connect to each other and to their bodies.

Trajectory treasure basket: Fill a basket with items that children can drop and throw such as feathers, leaves, fabric balls, petals and cotton wool.

Rotation treasure basket: Fill a basket with items that children can roll such as balls, pine cones, bangles and corks.

Enclosing treasure basket: Fill a basket with bangles, socks and lengths of fabric that children can use to enclose themselves and objects.

Enveloping treasure basket: Fill a basket with lots of different squares of fabric and loose parts for children to cover.

Positioning treasure basket: Fill a basket with different colored pom-poms and bowls for children to sort.

Transforming treasure basket: Fill a basket with lots of different sensory bottles. Children can explore how they transform when they shake them.

As children develop, adding an element of risk to loose parts play will support their listening and attention further. Opportunities such as woodwork, which can be made open-ended by allowing children to select resources independently, are a great example of this and require the child's full attention.

When looking at risk, it's always the decision of the setting as to how much risk they want to allow children to undertake during any activity and I would advise that you look into safety aspects of woodwork before implementing it. However, here is a budget-friendly way to implement starter woodwork with your cohort.

> *Visiting teachers first notice our children's depth of engagement. Some seem surprised that we introduce woodwork to such young children, but it is in fact a low-risk activity; I have been successfully doing it with pre-school children for many years.*

Pete Moorhouse (in 'Woodwork in the early years', 2015)

Woodwork starter activity

What you need

- Safety goggles

- Workbench or work mat

- Balsa wood

- Stubby hammer

- Nails

- Loose parts you can attach to the wood with nails (e.g. buttons, beads, cork, bottle tops)

What to do

It's important that this activity is undertaken in a quiet area with no distractions and that children wear safety goggles at all times. If you don't have a workbench I would suggest creating work mats (e.g. wood pieces or placemats) to avoid things being hammered into tables. When using the materials for the first time you may want to do this one to one, moving to higher adult to child ratios as they become more competent and confident.

For this activity, simply allow the children to practise hammering the nails into the balsa wood, securing loose parts as they wish. The children will not need much encouragement to come up with creative things to make but remember that the process is just as important, if not more important than the outcome.

UNDERSTANDING

When we look at the aspect of understanding we should think about young children beginning to understand gestures, single words and simple sentences. Moving forward, children will widen their understanding, developing concepts such as big and little and beginning to understand who, what and where questions. They will then move on to understanding how and why questions and the use of objects, in addition to responding during conversations.

There are lots of opportunities to develop understanding during play with loose parts – an environment rich with loose parts will be unbelievably rich with language. Loose parts, as opposed to man-made toys, offer a wealth of textures, scents, sounds and opportunities to discover. This means that we can widen the vocabulary of the children we teach just by enriching the environments we create.

For younger children, providing loose parts will introduce them to many sensory experiences. Natural resources in particular offer much more in the way of sensory experiences, as opposed to plastic that all looks and feels pretty much the same. And again, it's about enlarging vocabulary and introducing children to a wider range of words.

LOOKING FOR LEARNING: COMPARING LANGUAGE

During a discussion with a group of two- to four-year-olds they described a plastic ball using the following words:

- smooth
- round
- curved
- hard
- yellow
- bright

During a discussion with a group of two- to four-year-olds they described a pine cone using the following words:

- rough
- curved
- straight
- holey
- brown
- light brown
- damp
- sharp
- wonky
- hard
- spikey

When we introduce sensory experiences and treasure baskets to our very youngest children we need to think about all the language opportunities we are providing. We can see from the list on page 31 that the choices we make as practitioners have a huge impact on the language young children in our care will hear and begin to understand.

> *Recent research has shown that there is a significant gap between children with good and poor language skills when they begin school and that this gap remains consistent throughout their schooling.*
>
> **Padraic Monaghan (in 'Closing the word gap: What contributes to the variation in children's language development in the early years?', 2018)**

A key factor in this language gap is the number of words that a child hears during their early years and variety is also key to this. When we provide children with lots of natural and found loose parts we are able to open up a range of language. We must all ensure that we enrich the environment through our own language and, as practitioners, this means expanding our vocabulary instead of narrowly focusing on colours, shapes and amounts.

LOOKING FOR LEARNING:
COMPARING OBSERVATIONS

Observation one: A practitioner set up an activity where the children sorted plastic bears into big and small. All of the bears were either red, blue or yellow and came in two different sizes. Other than that, they were identical in shape, texture and scent.

The children began to sort the bears and the practitioner introduced language based around size: big, small, large, little, short and tall. The children spent a few minutes sorting the bears, with little discussion, before moving on to another activity of their choosing.

Observation two: A practitioner gathered a pot of bits and bobs collected from the environment and some different containers. The items included leaves, conkers, buttons and counters to name but a few.

The children started to sort the items into big and small. Child A placed all of the leaves in a big pile and all of the conkers in a small pile. Child B added buttons to the small pile. Child A stopped Child B and said, 'They're even smaller'. Child B replied, 'They're smaller than the leaves'. They continued to discuss this before making another pile of 'even smaller' items. Once sorted, the children began to compare the size of the leaves, noticing that the leaves were not the same size.

What are the children learning? Looking at the two observations above, we can see that both practitioners had set out to achieve the same thing. However, in the second observation the activity was much more open-ended and allowed for the children to talk more about shape, space and size, widening their vocabulary further than the first observation allowed for. Again, going back to my previous point, to extend the language of young children we must also widen our own vocabulary and be flexible about language.

SPEAKING

When we look at speaking in the early years, this aspect is about young children using their body language to share interests and beginning to use single words. As speech develops, children will use different types of words (nouns, verbs and adjectives) and begin to ask questions as they learn to use speech as a way to hold conversations, find out the meaning of their wider world and to engage in imaginative play.

As discussed in the previous aspects, we can create language-rich environments through our own vocabulary, alongside a wealth of loose parts with different textures, scents, colours and patterns. Loose parts also provide lots of opportunities for our youngest children to develop different types of words as they explore loose parts through schematic play.

	ROTATING	TRAJECTORY	POSITIONING	ENVELOPING
Nouns	spinning	lines	grouping	covering
Verbs	roll	move	build	contain
Adjectives	round	straight	tall	hidden
Preposition	across	along	under	inside

Introducing this variety of words through the children's play and interests will help them to understand how things work and engage them in conversations about how and why things work as they develop their speech.

Furthermore, loose parts are a simple addition to enhance language during imaginative play because we are able to provide children with open-ended resources that don't limit their imaginations. For example, a princess dressing-up outfit can only be a princess dress but a long piece of blue fabric can be many different things depending on the child using it: a princess dress, a body of water, a base for transient art, a blanket and much more.

Deconstructed role play

Deconstructed role play gives children the opportunity to create their own play. Instead of spending hours creating a post office or a castle, you can simply give children the resources they need to create whatever sparks their imagination. Children will talk throughout the whole process as they create and construct the role play right up to inviting other children to share in the experience. There are lots of other benefits for using deconstructed role play. Children will think critically, be creative, access many other areas of development, gain independence and much more.

What you need:

You can add an array of loose parts to your deconstructed role play area. When starting out, add lots of boxes, lengths of fabric, small tyres, crates and cable reels. Children can add other loose parts from around the environment as they're needed. Over time you will find that the area naturally transforms as children add and remove items.

What to do:

It's essential that you give children time and space to allow their role play and storytelling to evolve. Sometimes children will need help with their constructions or want you to play along and you should follow the cues of the child to become an effective play partner.

Although we want to encourage language, try to interact rather than questioning everything that's going on.

Conclusion

When looking at loose parts play in relation to communication and language we can see, as with personal, social and emotional development, that it's very much the ethos of loose parts play that we are concerned with. When children are able to follow their own line of enquiry they will be more engaged, and therefore their language will flourish because they will have an active interest. It's also important that we bridge the language gap by using a wealth of language during play, looking particularly at the variety of words we expose young children to.

Physical development

During this chapter about physical development we are going to look at the two strands outlined in the early years statutory framework. Firstly, there is the moving and handling aspect which is all about developing gross and fine motor skills. Secondly, we will look at the health and self-care aspect which is about children becoming independent – a key skill they will need when they begin school.

Something we have already discussed in this book is that loose parts play isn't just about resources; it's an ethos that encompasses every area of learning. Although you will see more resource-led ideas for the specific areas of learning, for the prime areas it's a lot more about our attitudes towards young children and their learning. Our attitudes are what will form the basis for good practice when it comes to loose parts play in action.

MOVING AND HANDLING

For younger children moving and handling is about those early physical movements: reaching out, holding items, rolling, crawling and so on. As children progress they will begin to develop their physical skills further as they climb, balance and jump. They will also begin to develop their fine motor skills which are essential for all areas of learning.

A prerequisite for any environment tailored to babies is that there is lots of space for them to practise their physical movements and lots of interesting loose parts that are safe for them to interact with. This includes resources that are safe for sucking and mouthing, especially during the stage when children explore materials mainly through their senses. Many practitioners fear the use of loose parts within baby room environments due to the risks associated with them. However, I hope that by now we can all agree that there are lots of loose parts that are safe for babies and this should not be a barrier to their use and enjoyment.

Loose parts for babies

- Blocks of different sizes, shape and texture
- Material cut into varying lengths and widths and in different fabrics
- Various types of paper and card
- Cardboard boxes and tubes
- Biscuit and chocolate tins
- Large bottle tops and lids
- Bangles
- Large balls in different textures
- Home-made edible play dough
- Non-toxic shaving foam
- Large natural materials such as large shells, pebbles and pine cones
- Wooden utensils
- Different types of sponges and cloths

An environment filled with lot of interesting, open-ended resources for babies to engage with will encourage them to reach out, grasp, roll and crawl. Exploring treasure baskets will allow young children to handle many different items: to roll, throw and squeeze objects as they explore them.

Another thing to remember is that everything we provide for children needs to be at their level and that includes those who cannot yet walk. These babies will only be able to access items within their reach from the floor which is why it's important to provide lots of stations on the floor for them to explore.

Different types of treasure baskets			
Metal	Wood	Fabric	Brushes/sponges
• utensils	• utensils	• sequin	• hairbrush
• colander	• egg cup	• chiffon	• nail brush
• tea strainer	• curtain hoops	• cotton	• body brush
• cookie cutters	• bangles	• organza	• sponge
	• bobbins	• fleece	
	• balls	• flannel	

Nature station set up

Nature is all around us and lots of it is freely available: pine cones, fallen leaves, petals, sticks and let's not forget things we can pick up from the supermarket such as seasonal fruits and vegetables.

What you need:

- A rug or platform

- Natural loose parts: this might be sprouts in the winter or leaves in the autumn

- Ramps/tubes/baskets

What to do:

- Using the rug or platform as your station, add the natural loose parts to it. You can be as creative as you want or simply add them to a basket on the rug.

- Provide resources to extend exploration such as ramps for rolling things along, tubes for filling and emptying or baskets for transporting the loose parts.

- Encourage children to handle the objects and explore how they can grasp, throw and move the items using thier bodies.

Obstacle set up

Setting up small obstacles at a child's level will allow them to practise those larger movements: pulling themselves up, climbing over things, crawling onto a step and so on.

What you need:

- Low platform

- Tyres

- Sturdy boxes

- Cushions

- Large loose parts

What to do:

- Allow children to climb onto, over and inside the different objects; pulling themselves up and taking risks.

- Place the cushions around the large loose parts as an extra precaution. However, you may find that the children want to explore these, lifting them into the boxes and tyres.

Loose parts play is particularly good for developing risk awareness during physical play, especially for children who enjoy lots of active learning. Providing lots of large scrap materials will allow young children to develop physical skills such as lifting, climbing, balancing and jumping alongside being creative and developing many other skills at the same time. When I meet practitioners with a boy-heavy cohort many of them have similar stories; that they cannot get their boys to engage in other areas of learning during free play because they're too busy accessing the outdoor area and being active. This is where we, as skilled practitioners, need to build other areas of learning into physical play, as well as recognising that active play does include lots of areas of learning, e.g. den building requires lots of communication, negotiation, sharing and turn taking, in addition to lots of mathematical thinking as children choose the correct shapes, lengths and materials for the job.

Children will also use creative and critical thinking skills and let's not forget those all-important physical skills that this chapter is all about. It can be easy for practitioners to focus on the obvious learning that's taking place during certain activities. Spending time properly observing play and reflecting on the areas of learning will allow practitioners to notice more learning is taking place than that they first thought or that's most obvious.

Large scrap materials

Providing a large space outdoors with lots of larger loose parts will give children the opportunity to use their imagination to construct dens, boats, spaceships and much more. Children love the element of risk associated with this type of play and it's sure to engage even the most active children.

What you need:

- A large space
- Cable reels
- Tyres
- Crates
- Tarpaulin
- Planks of wood
- Tubes

What to do:

- Allow children to explore the materials freely; working together and using their critical thinking skills to create something.

- When children come up against obstacles, allow them to problem solve by communicating and negotiating, stepping in only when necessary.

- The children will think about what shapes they need for their structures, which items will fit together and discover ways to develop their structures further.

It's important to remember that physical development and loose parts play isn't just about large scrap materials, there are also lots of ways that children can develop their fine motor skills especially when we enhance the play with purposeful resources, such as including jugs in water play for children to practise pouring or by adding small spoons to the sand play for digging. Simply by handling small resources during activities such as transient art, children will be developing fine motor skills as they begin to use their finger and thumb as a pincer to pick up items, position and balance them.

Transient art

Transient art is a simple way to invite young children to be creative. Its most crucial benefit is the opportunity it provides to create and recreate. The parts can be changed if put in the wrong place, and therefore children don't have to worry about making mistakes.

What you need:

- Small loose parts: this might be anything from bottle tops and buttons to pipe cleaners and old board game pieces

- A base for the transient art: you could use tiles, frames, squares of fabric or simply a tabletop

- Tweezers/spoons/chopsticks

What to do:

- Allow the children to use the small loose parts to create pictures, shapes and patterns on their base.

- When first starting out with transient art, provide prompts and model creating transient pictures.

- You can use an interest to encourage children to create such as providing mirrors and asking them to make a self-portrait. But remember that children should be able to follow whatever direction they choose.

- To further develop fine motor skills you could add tweezers, spoons or chopsticks to encourage the children to try to pick up the small loose parts in different ways.

Transient structures

Transient structures are the same concept as transient art. I first came across transient structures when one little boy followed his own ideas and stacked up log slices to create a 'Christmas tree' which he decorated with glass beads and bamboo cuttings.

What you need:

- Small loose parts: pom-poms, glass beads, bolts, etc.

- Medium loose parts: this might be log slices, short tubes, blocks and cardboard boxes

What to do:

- As with transient art, allow children to be creative and make structures with the items.

- On this larger scale, you can encourage children to work together to create something.

- Children will gain an understanding about balance, as well as many other concepts such as shape, space and measure.

HEALTH AND SELF-CARE

When looking at health and self-care and its links to loose parts play it's the ethos of loose parts play that has a role in this aspect of development. It's about children being given the confidence, freedom and independence to learn to look after themselves: to hold a cup, to feed themselves, to get their own coats and to use the toilet. Just by providing lots of loose parts and open-ended materials we are giving children independence in their choices, thereby building their confidence and making them aware that the environment is theirs and can be used as they please.

Think about how you give children independence to do simple things such as accessing their belongings. If children's coats and bags are in another room or out of reach this will not only create more work for the adults but will limit the children's independence. How can children be expected to learn to put their own coats, gloves, hats and wellies on if every time they go outside an adult retrieves them all quickly and does everything for them to enable everyone to get outside as quickly as possible? Putting on coats and wellies shouldn't be seen as a chore but as a learning opportunity, especially for those children (with busy parents) who may rarely be given these opportunities at home.

Patience is a key skill when it comes to creating an environment that nurtures children's independence. I can't even begin to imagine how many times a child has spilt a drink all over the table, dropped their fork during lunch or put their wellies on the wrong feet and although it's easy for us to take over, why not allow children to rectify these things for themselves? During lunchtime, think about providing spare cutlery within the room. If a child drops a fork they can put it in the dirty bowl and retrieve a clean one without an adult having to do anything. This is the same when children pour their own water. Make sure there are paper towels and mops available should a child need to clean up after themselves. Think about where else this may be useful such as by the water play, within the art area and during messy play. Children never quite clean up properly but they're trying and they're being given the confidence to try – that's what's important.

Conclusion

We can see that loose parts themselves provide many opportunities for developing gross and fine motor skills, taking away the need for overly-planned activities to enhance physical development. More importantly, the ethos of loose parts play gives children the confidence to be independent and to learn key health and self-care skills.

LOOKING FOR LEARNING:
I CAN GET MY WELLIES

Observation: I watched a boy as he took off his shoes and placed them neatly under his peg. He reached up to get a bag off his peg but couldn't quite reach. He looked around the room. He then went down to the toilets and retrieved a step which he placed under his peg, stood on it and retrieved the bag. He got his wellies out and put them on his feet before confidently striding outside.

What are the children learning? It would have taken me less than a minute to get the child's wellies and put them on his feet rather than the ten minutes it took him to do it on his own. But what are we teaching children when we do it for them? All we are showing them, by interfering, is that we can do it more quickly and that it's easier if adults do everything for them. Instead this little boy, given the space and time to do it himself, had a sense of achievement as he was able to independently access his belongings without help.

Literacy

There are lots of ways that loose parts and open-ended materials can be used to develop literacy skills (reading and writing) if we provide the right resources within our environments. Throughout this chapter we will look at lots of different ways of creating a literacy-rich environment alongside the loose parts provided.

READING

When looking at reading, this is all about introducing stories, books and rhymes from an early age. As children develop their reading skills they will be able to retell stories and make up their own as well as building their phonic knowledge to enable them to read simple words.

Throughout this chapter you will find, providing your environment is filled with loose parts and scrap materials to begin with, that lots of these opportunities already exist. Sometimes, due to being activity conditioned, practitioners don't recognise development that's happening and therefore this book is focussed on ideas that you can implement straight away. We must remember throughout that these are ideas and shouldn't be used as an adult-directed task or activity, instead follow the children's lead and support their thoughts and ideas. As discussed in the 'Introducing loose parts' chapter, loose parts play is about complete freedom and choice but, as practitioners, that doesn't mean we cannot guide or tailor our environments to develop certain skills as long as we are flexible about it.

- If we are looking at reading with babies in mind then you should be thinking about:

- introducing them to books and rhymes from a young age

- allowing them to handle books and respond to stories by giving them opportunities to point and interact with parts that interest them.

Creating spaces for young children to relax and enjoy books in a supportive environment is important. Think about creating a cosy corner with lots of blankets and cushions. Consider the colours and resources you provide in this area to ensure that they don't distract from the books and stories. Books should also be available at the child's level to allow them to interact with books freely. Practitioners should take notice of when children access the area so they can support them, especially babies when they're exploring books.

You can introduce loose parts play alongside books by adding different fabrics, natural and scrap materials which will bring stories to life, e.g. you may provide different fabrics to represent the textures of different animals in a story or you could create storytelling spaces outdoors so that children can experience a book about a particular season whilst being surrounded by it. As children get older they will use their imaginations to select loose parts for storytelling, but for babies we can put together story sacks to go with different books. This is also a great way to introduce loose parts play for the first time with children of any age but the older the child, the more open-ended the story sack should be.

Story sack for babies

A story sack for babies should include lots of sensory items that represent characters or scenes within the story so that children can experience the story through their senses. You can add fabrics that represent the texture of animals, real objects that represent ones in the story such as flowers and grass. It doesn't have to just be a sack, you could provide bowls filled with loose parts for children to explore.

We're Going on a Bear Hunt by Michael Rosen and Helen Oxenbury

What you need:

- Bowls filled with water, mud, grass, sticks and snow (you could use cotton wool) to represent the different scenes

What to do:

- Allow young children to explore the different textures, scents and sounds as they play with the materials.

- Water and mud are great loose parts that children will manipulate and explore in many different ways.

Story sack for two-year-olds

As children develop further they will want to explore how and why things happen. Books that tap into a child's schema will engage them in a story. You can use books about making potions for children exploring transformation or books about cars for children exploring a trajectory schema; providing loose parts for combining or throwing, retrospectively, alongside the book.

The Very Busy Spider by Eric Carle

What you need:

- Items for spinning: spinning tops, balls, bottle tops, CDs, plastic eggs, etc.

What to do:

- Read the story with the children, encouraging them to spin an item in turn every time the story says 'spin' or 'spinning'.

- Allow the children to talk about how the items spin.

- Once you have read the book, encourage children to explore it with the items within your continuous provision.

Story sack for preschool children

Finally, as children develop, you can provide books with a selection of loose parts to give them complete freedom. Providing natural loose parts with both fiction and non-fiction is a great way to stimulate thoughts and ideas.

A Nest is Noisy by Dianna Hutts Aston and Sylvia Long

What you need:

- Natural loose parts: sticks, leaves, grass and feathers

- Eggs: plastic, wooden, etc.

What to do:

- Introduce the book to the children, always trying to find a time when an interest has naturally occurred, e.g. when children show a fascination with birds or a nest appears in the outdoor area.

- Add the book to your continuous provision with the loose parts and simply allow the children to use the items as they please.

- Some children will sort the items, others will create their own nests and many children will do something completely unexpected.

We can also offer books in different areas of our provision rather than one designated book area. This means that we can provide a wealth of different books when and where they're relevant for young children. Although I don't advocate specific areas you will find that the children naturally create areas through their play that you can add books to in line with their ideas. For example, place books about building in the block play area or books about colour with the painting resources, thereby engaging children with books that are relevant to them and their play ideas.

Finally, there are lots of books specifically about loose parts and loose parts play to enhance creativity and imagination. These are also another great resource when introducing loose parts for the first time:

Loose parts books

- *Not a Box* and *Not a Stick* by Antoinette Portis introduce children to all the wonderful things a box or a stick can be with a little bit of imagination.

- *Roxaboxen* by Alice McLerran and Barbara Cooney shows that with some imagination even a rocky hill can become a magical place.

- *Leaf Man* by Lois Ehlert is about a man made of leaves that travels with the wind.

- *Stanley's Stick* by John Hegley and Neal Layton shows you all the things you can do with just a stick.

- *If You Find a Rock* by Peggy Christian and Barbara Hirsch Lember shows children that a rock isn't just a rock.

- *Let's Make Faces* by Hanoch Piven shows children how they can find faces in everyday objects with buttons for eyes and hooks for noses.

As children develop their reading skills, they will begin to show an interest in letters and their own name. There are lots of resources we can provide alongside loose parts to encourage and extend this interest.

Transient art name cards

There are lots of ways to encourage children to use loose parts to explore letters and their names. In our setting, amongst the other bases we have available for transient art, we also have cardboard rectangles with the children's names on that they can use.

What you need:

- Small loose parts: pom-poms, buttons, beads, etc.

- Cardboard name boards (simply write each child's name on a rectangular piece of cardboard)

What to do:

- Children can explore the letters in their name by recreating the letter shapes using loose parts.

- Practitioners can support children's learning by sounding out different letters, encouraging children to take notice of the first sound in their name.

- Children are naturally curious about their own names and how they're similar to others. They will want to talk about who else has the same letters as them in their names.

- You can further extend discussions by talking about what objects in the room have the same initial sound as the children's names.

Creating letters

This idea is about encouraging children to take notice of letters and how they're formed. It also gives children an opportunity to see the shapes of letters of significance to them, such as the letters in their name. You can create letters in many different ways, but I find that children enjoy using play dough, clay and other malleable materials to explore letters.

What you need:

- Wooden letters (you can print out letters, but tangible letters allow them to explore how the shapes feel)

- Play dough

- Rolling pins

- Scissors

What to do:

- Children can select a wooden letter to replicate using play dough.

- Forming the letters will give children opportunities to build their fine motor skills as they manipulate the dough into the shapes they want.

- Practitioners can model how to make basic shapes with the dough such as how to roll a sausage shape or a ball.

- By providing other resources, such as rolling pins and scissors, children may approach the letter making in different ways.

Think about enhancing sand play by hiding wooden letters in the sand or try adding log slices with engraved letters to your construction play. There are lots of ways to incorporate letters into the environment even if it's just to spark an interest by having them make an appearance.

LOOKING FOR LEARNING:
EAT YOUR 'A'

Observation: I observed a couple of children playing with dolls. They decided it was time to make the dolls some dinner and went over to the kitchen. They retrieved a pan that had already been filled with lots of random objects and started to 'cook' the contents. They split the contents into two bowls and began to feed the dolls. One of the children found a wooden 'a' in their food which they 'fed' to the doll and said, 'Eat your 'a''. The other child hurriedly looked through their bowl to see if they had any letters and found an 'm'. The child picked it up and said, 'What's this one?', the other child said, 'It's an 'm''. They then continued to look for letters and questioned each other about what letters they had found.

What are the children learning? This is an example of how letters within the environment can spark off a whole child-directed activity around letters. Admittedly, the children's knowledge of letters was limited and not everything they discussed was correct but at the time it was simply important that they had an interest.

WRITING

When looking at writing for our youngest children, it's all about building their communication and language skills. However, as children get older they will begin to make marks through drawings and paintings that they ascribe a meaning to. As children develop their writing skills further they will learn to link sounds to letters and begin to write their own names and other simple words.

Although your youngest children won't yet ascribe a meaning to the marks they make during messy play, such as finger painting and mark making in sand, it's still great practice for developing those all-important fine motor skills that will be needed when they begin to paint and draw. All malleable materials are loose parts which can be used in many different ways by many different children; they can be manipulated, combined, transported and transformed by the little hands that explore them all whilst developing gross and fine motor skills.

As children develop, they will start to make marks that do have a meaning (even if these marks aren't recognisable to practitioners). Children will draw people and objects of interest to them. Drawing and painting are all forms of loose parts play as children can imagine and create anything. This is why they should be given freedom to explore these mediums without an outcome. Instead of saying, 'Let's draw our family' or 'Let's paint a house' why not simply say, 'Let's draw' or 'Let's paint', thereby allowing children the freedom to create whatever they want? It's also important to write down what children say when they explain their pictures to you and to attach it to their masterpieces – this shows them that speech can be turned into marks.

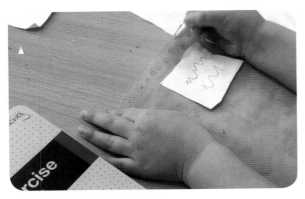

Another important area of literacy is the ability to decode words using phonics. When looking at this area, loose parts offer children the opportunity to explore a wealth of sounds due to the varying shapes, textures and scents of all the different open-ended materials that are part of it.

If we think back to the variation of words used to describe a plastic ball and a pine cone (page 31), it's clear to see that loose parts can be incredibly powerful when it comes to enhancing language which is crucial for developing phonics. There are loose parts and materials all around us that need little to no budget at all. Even better they need no forward planning and children are extremely curious about them. Take nature as an example, children love to talk about nature because it's relevant to their everyday lives. Children can feel the rain, see the clouds and smell the grass; what better way, for both practitioners and children, to develop those early phonetic skills than by accessing the abundance of opportunities that nature provides.

Nature sounds
. . . .
What better way to explore sounds than through those found in nature – sounds that are all around us.

What you need:

- A natural outdoor space is all you need

What to do:

- Talk to the children about what good listening is.

- Sit in or walk around the outdoor space and ask the children to listen to the sounds around them: what can they hear? Where is the noise coming from? Is the sound loud, quiet, fast, slow?

- Alternatively, you can bring natural materials indoors and ask the children to close their eyes and guess what the sound is, e.g. crunching leaves or clapping conkers together.

Conclusion
Loose parts play provides many opportunities for creating a love of reading by providing resources to accompany storybooks that will allow children who cannot read to continue their explorations of stories without an adult. Loose parts also play an integral role when it comes to learning sounds and just providing letters throughout the environment will spark an interest in literacy.

Mathematics

Mathematics can be split into two aspects: number; and shape, space and measure. What better way to introduce and develop mathematical concepts than through loose parts which give children lots of opportunities for counting, weighing, sorting, measuring and much more. Loose parts play also gives children opportunities to problem solve and to gain an understanding that maths can be approached in many different ways.

NUMBER

Younger children will develop an awareness of numbers through stories and rhymes. As they develop, children will begin to use number names randomly and begin to sort objects. This will progress to children being able to recite numbers in order, use mathematical language, compare quantities and select specific amounts. As they build up their knowledge of number, children will start to count objects, select quantities and begin to understand simple addition and subtraction.

An environment filled with loose parts will provide many opportunities for exploring number. Babies will explore the existence of objects through treasure baskets and schematic play by holding and exploring a small number of objects, e.g. two shells or three sticks and by hiding objects under pieces of material, baskets and containers. As younger children develop further, loose parts will give them lots of opportunities to sort items. Instead of setting up a sorting activity or providing resources for that purpose, children will be able to sort natural materials such as leaves, flowers, sticks, shells and stones into an array of different containers such as wicker baskets, large tins, bowls and bags. Specifically-made maths resources can be expensive, whereas environments based around loose parts enable children to explore number using freely- or cheaply-available natural and scrap resources. Creating maths stations will invite children to explore number using loose parts within your setting.

Colour sorting station

You can create a colour sorting station with just about anything from bottle tops and leaves to pom-poms.

What you need:

- Different coloured objects to sort
- Containers to sort into: this might be baskets, tins or bowls
- Tweezers
- Spoons

What to do:

- Set out the different coloured objects and the containers. You can add tweezers or spoons to target fine motor skills too.

- Allow the children to sort the objects in any way that they want. Some will sort each colour into a separate container, others will sort one of each colour into separate containers and others might sort the blues and greens away from the rest of the colours.

- Remember loose parts are open-ended and children can choose to sort in any way that they want, even if it doesn't appear logical to adults.

Number exploration station

You can choose to create a number station in one area of your continuous provision or add different aspects of this idea to different spaces throughout your indoor and outdoor environments.

What you need:

- Numbers: wooden, mirror, plastic, etc.
- Containers with numbers written on
- Lots of loose parts

What to do:

- Adding tangible numbers to your continuous provision will spark an interest in number. You can hide them in sand, place them in a bowl or attach them to containers to see what children might do.

- Some children will count out loose parts in containers and others may simply add the numbers to their creations as decoration. Either way, children will be exploring and interacting with numbers.

- Skilled practitioners should think about appropriate ways to implement number into other areas of children's play, ensuring it's in line with what they're doing. When children are talking about how many buttons they need for their art you may want to add the actual numbers to the table to spark more discussions around number and counting.

We can encourage children to explore number through their interests. Think about how number can be implemented within different parts of your play space. Children can count out how many stones they add to their mud pies or how many crates they need to build a den – the possibilities are endless and don't require hours of planning or adult-directed activities. You simply need an abundance of loose parts and open-ended materials that inspire children to take an interest and engage.

As with many aspects of loose parts play, it requires skilled practitioners who can follow the child's line of enquiry. If we try to take over during a child's play and start to randomly talk about number, questioning children on everything we can, they will lose interest. Instead it's about understanding their thoughts and ideas and how we can extend these.

LOOKING FOR LEARNING:
NUMBER TUBES IN THE CONSTRUCTION AREA

Ever since we introduced number tubes to the construction area we have been blown away by how many children have been using mathematical language to describe their creations and they have become our must-have resource for many areas of continuous provision. Although a great addition regardless of what the children do, we originally added these based on the children's lines of enquiry.

Observation: We noticed that many of the boys in our setting were using loose parts to create structures and this became a daily occurrence. Although in itself there were many different types of development happening, we noticed that the children's priority was to build the tallest tower. Through careful observations we noticed that many of the children's conversations involved discussing who had made the 'biggest' tower.

Based on this observation, we added number tubes to extend their discussions and to encourage them to count out how tall their towers were. This led to further discussions about how to make a tower 'four tall' or 'four wide'.

What are the children learning? This is an example of how looking deeper at children's play can help practitioners to extend the learning in a direction that's meaningful and relevant to the child. When we extend play in the direction a child is taking it we find that they're much more engaged and likely to follow our extensions.

SHAPE, SPACE AND MEASURE

Shape, space and measure for babies is the awareness of objects through their senses, observing and touching objects to gain an understanding of shape, size and weight. As children develop, they will begin to understand big and small, explore how items fit within other items and gain an idea of space by filling and emptying.

As children further develop their mathematical skills they will begin to categorise items based on their size and shape, use positional language, select appropriate shapes for their play and talk about shapes generally. By the end of the early years, children will be able to order small numbers of objects by weight, length or height, be able to describe relative position and begin to use 3D shape names.

Loose parts are the best way to develop an understanding of shape, space and measure as you fill their environment with curious objects of varying properties that children can explore. Again, as with number, we can set up lots of stations for children to explore shape, space and measure.

Weighing and measuring station

· · · · · · · ·

You can choose to create a weighing station in one area of your continuous provision or add different aspects of this idea to different spaces throughout your indoor and outdoor environments.

What you need:

- Weighing scales
- Measuring cups
- Measuring spoons
- Rulers
- Lots of loose parts

What to do:

- You can add all of these items to one station within your environment or provide various items in different areas within your continuous provision, e.g. scales in the role play area and measuring cups with the play dough.

- Children can use the station to explore how much an item weighs or measures, learning to use the appropriate resource for the task.

- For younger children, you can measure how many sticks long something is or how many beads long something is.

- Practitioners can encourage children to find items that are heavier, lighter, longer or shorter than the previous. They can test out if they're right by using the relevant resource to weigh or measure.

Comparing size

Loose parts are great for making comparisons because they're so varied and one child's comparison may not be the same as another child's.

What you need:

- Roll of paper
- Sticks
- Leaves
- Pine cones
- Container

What to do:

- Roll out the paper and write 'small' at one end and 'big' at the other. You may want to place the biggest item you have at the big end and the smallest at the small end as a starting point for the children.

- Place the sticks, leaves and pine cones in a container.

- Explain to the children that they're going to arrange the items in order of size from small to big. Allow the children to select an item from the container and place it along the line.

- As the children place items, there will be discussions as items may need to be moved further along to create space for other items.

- Comparing natural items will lead to more discussion: a leaf may be smaller than another leaf widthways but bigger lengthways. This is when children will use their critical thinking skills to decide how to approach the task.

Children will also be exploring concepts of shape, space and measure through everything that they do from creating with clay to building dens. It's the job of each practitioner to take notice of what children are engaged in from more than just a physical viewpoint by delving a bit deeper and trying to understand what a child is thinking.

LOOKING FOR LEARNING: DEN BUILDING

Den building appeals to many children – the element of risk associated with it and the excitement of creating a hiding place ensures this. There is lots of learning going on, particularly physical development, which can sometimes outshine all the mathematical thinking that's happening.

Observation: I observed four boys as they started to create a den with the large loose parts in the outdoor area. The boys discussed what they needed and some of the items named were 'two tyres', 'some big pegs', 'a long pole' and 'four seats'. As the boys built their den they talked about what would fit where and commented on their den, 'That won't be big enough', 'Will it fit four chairs in?' and 'I need a smaller tyre'.

What are the children learning? Often, when we observe den building we automatically categorise it as physical development or even personal, social and emotional development. In fact, if we listen and observe closely we can see that there is lots of mathematical language and problem solving happening throughout the process.

There are also many opportunities to explore mathematics in your outdoor environment: looking at the different shapes nature has to offer, the wealth of patterns and all the comparisons that we can make between the simplest of objects such as leaves, stones and flowers. It offers more opportunities for discussion and problem solving than an environment that relies on plastic bears and counters to develop mathematical thinking. Try adding a mud kitchen or potion station to your outdoor area to invite children to engage in mathematical thinking.

Mud kitchen

A mud kitchen is a great way to use all those wonderful loose parts that nature has to offer: sticks, petals, leaves, twigs, mud, sand and stones make wonderful mud pies and leaf teas. With the addition of a few simple resources you can maximise the mathematics that takes place.

What you need:

- Mud kitchen: this can be as simple as a couple of crates with a plank of wood across them

- Old pots/pans and kitchen utensils

- Loose parts from the outdoor environment: leaves, sticks, petals, etc.

- Weighing scales

- Measuring jugs/spoons and cups

What to do:

- Children will come up with lots of creative ways to combine the natural materials to create pies, teas and soups – experimenting with amounts to create different consistencies.

- Younger children can measure out ingredients in terms of handfuls or spoonfuls, whereas older children can use the measuring jugs for more specific amounts.

- Practitioners can create simple recipes, again thinking of the age group. For younger children it will be a simple recipe (two cups of water, two cups of sand, three leaves) and for older children it will be a more advanced recipe (100ml of water, two cups of sand, 10g of leaves).

- You can encourage children to create their own recipes by writing one out before using the mud kitchen or writing it as they go along. Practitioners may model this for younger children.

Conclusion

We can see that when looking at mathematics it's about ignoring outdated views of what maths should look like in practice and, instead, embracing all the mathematical concepts children can explore just by handling, playing with and exploring loose parts.

Understanding the world

Understanding the world is made up of three aspects: people and communities, the world, and technology. There are lots of ways that loose parts can help in the development of these areas for young children, from being used in deconstructed role play to taking pictures of their transient art.

PEOPLE AND COMMUNITIES

Our youngest children develop their understanding of people and communities through forming attachments and creating bonds. As they develop, children will begin to role play aspects of their everyday lives, make friends and talk about different occupations. Loose parts have a key role in this area of development as they give children the freedom to select resources freely for their play.

When thinking about our youngest children, their thoughts and ideas surrounding differences are created based on their experiences. An example of this is how some types of play are viewed negatively compared to others, e.g. children who like boisterous play are often branded as 'naughty', whereas the child who enjoys sitting quietly is 'good'. Children will notice that these types of play are viewed differently by adults and this will influence their ideas about good and bad behaviour. Additionally, practitioners might set up activities with a specific gender in mind such as cars for boys. There is absolutely nothing wrong with this if you find that a lot of the boys in your setting enjoy cars but let's not forget about the boys who don't want to play with cars or the girls who want to play with cars. This is why loose parts and a flexible environment provide more opportunities for children to express themselves positively. As discussed earlier in the book, we need

to make space for all types of play and that's what a flexible environment looks like. Environments filled with loose parts take away the need for stereotypical toys because they offer so much more in the way of learning – children can create their own resources.

Another point to remember is that what our home looks like may be very different from what a child's home looks like. Deconstructed role play allows children to create what they want their home to look like rather than this being predetermined by an adult. This extends the learning to a whole new level as children build up the role play, engage with others to create their home and add items that are meaningful and represent something to them.

LOOKING FOR LEARNING:
LET'S BUILD A CAMPSITE

When watching young children role play, their imaginations are what makes it special. Loose parts play will ensure that their imaginations aren't limited by the resources you provide.

Observation: I observed a child as she made a camp fire. She collected logs and put them in a pile in the middle of the floor. She then placed cushions in a circle around the logs and added a basket which she said was a tent. Once this was set up, she told her friends to come and sit at the camp fire, announcing that she was going to make some food. She collected some large wooden circles which she handed out to each child. 'There's a plate for you', she said as she handed one out. She collected some sticks which she held over the camp fire and then gave each child one and said, 'Eat your sausages'.

What are the children learning? This example shows us that by providing loose parts and open-ended resources children are able to engage in play that practitioners might not have thought of. I later found out that the camp fire idea had come from home. The girl's older brother had been camping with scouts and had told her all about the trip. The loose parts meant that she could role play these ideas immediately.

Just like the experiences children have at home, as people we are also all completely unique. When investigating ourselves or others, loose parts play gives children the ability to recreate people with all their uniqueness. For example, quite often children are asked to create self-portraits of themselves at the beginning of the academic year. This usually involves a piece of paper per child and paints that represent different skin, eye and hair colours. Children are a lot more perceptive than we give them credit for. A little boy told me that his skin is peach, one of his friends is peachy white and his other friend is white with no peach, so why limit this by providing one paint colour to represent all these differing skin tones? This is why loose parts are so special. Children can select their own resources with no limitations. Try out the family portraits idea opposite and see just how creative children can be.

Family portraits

What better way to create portraits than through loose parts where children can make similarities between everyday objects and faces.

What you need:

- A base: this might be a round placemat or circular piece of paper

- Small loose parts: the more you can provide the better, anything from buttons to matchsticks, bottle tops to lollipop sticks

- Photographs of each child's family

What to do:

- Give children the opportunity to explore the different materials available to them. You can discuss some of the similarities as a group, such as how many eyes the children will need for their portraits.

- Model creating your own family portrait, talking about what you're using and why. You might say, 'I'm using blue buttons for my eyes because my eyes are blue' or, 'I need lots of pipe cleaners because I have lots of hair'. This will encourage children to think about the materials they use and to share that with the group.

- Remember to keep the process open-ended and allow children to make their own choices even if they choose not to make a face at all.

THE WORLD

When we look at understanding the world, loose parts lend themselves really well to this aspect of development. We can use treasure baskets and scrap resources to give children opportunities to explore schemas – a huge source of learning when it comes to thinking about how and why things work.

In addition, children will develop an understanding of the natural world and observe the changing seasons, plants, animals and insects. Natural loose parts are accessible and can even be collected by children, making this the perfect way to explore nature.

For our youngest children, we need an environment that fosters schema exploration and resources that allow children to explore how things work and how they can impact on the world around them.

Sensory schema play

Providing babies and young children with loose parts that engage their schematic impulses will develop their understanding of the world. As children engage in schema play, watching and listening to adults, they will focus their attention in order to make sense of the world and how things work. Try providing the following sensory play idea into your continuous provision.

Connection sensory play: Add funnels, pipes and tubes to water, sand or foam play.

Trajectory sensory play: Blow bubbles for babies to observe and touch.

Rotation sensory play: Roll balls through different mediums – paint, sand and mud all work well.

Enclosing sensory play: Add blocks to sand play to create enclosures.

Transporting sensory play: Add sponges and containers to water play.

Positioning sensory play: Add loose parts to malleable materials such as clay and play dough.

Transforming sensory play: Mix different mediums together, such as water and sand or shaving foam and glitter.

Enveloping sensory play: Hide loose parts in shaving foam or play dough.

Orientation sensory play: Add a mirror to the bottom of tuff trays and fill with leaves.

As children further develop their understanding, they will continue to use loose parts and open-ended materials for a purpose and extend their thoughts and ideas, using what they already know. Again, this becomes a very creative experience for children rather than following prescribed steps. This can be seen when a child, for example, uses glue. The first time a child is introduced to glue they will saturate the paper, often using more glue than is required as they explore the medium. As a child gets older they will understand that they only need a thin layer of glue to make things stick. They will then begin to use what they know and attempt to glue other things together, sometimes successfully and other times not so successfully but each time they will gain a little bit more knowledge.

Tinker station

Create a tinker station for children to explore different loose parts and materials. This will give children an opportunity to be curious about different materials and to find out for themselves how and why things happen.

What you need:

- Tinker tray (see tinker tray section on page 12 for ideas)
- Tweezers
- Rulers
- Weighing scales
- Magnifying glasses
- Scissors

What to do:

- Allow children to freely tinker and explore the loose parts available. They might explore how they differ from one another or what their similarities are.

- They may combine the loose parts, measure them or cut them open.

- Practitioners can support children by listening to their discoveries and documenting their thoughts.

Through natural loose parts we can introduce the children to nature by talking about where the loose parts come from. This is a great tool for educating them about the importance of nature and our impact on the environment. Providing an abundance of natural loose parts indoors as well as outdoors will show children the endless possibilities nature has to offer. This will help children understand that nature is a crucial part of our lives and encourage them to value it. Furthermore, nature provides us with the best shapes, textures, patterns and colours. We can use all of these to engage the children in conversations about how and why.

Nature sorting

Just by giving children lots of opportunities to get outside, they will instinctively explore nature. If you don't have a particularly natural outdoor environment think of ways you can include nature by adding natural loose parts as well as by planting flowers, herbs and shrubs throughout the continuous provision. This might be in designated beds or pots depending on the space available to you. Alternatively, find a local park or woodland to explore with the children. The following idea can be adapted depending on the area you're exploring, and will encourage children to consider the many differences nature has to offer.

What you need:

- Colour paint swatches: you can pick these up for free from local hardware or DIY stores

- A base for sorting: this could be a tray with compartments or a piece of cardboard with elastic bands around it

What to do:

- Place different coloured swatches into the compartments of the tray or connect them to the cardboard using the elastic bands.

- Allow the children to collect items in the natural environment and to sort them by colour using their sorting base.

- For younger children you can provide limited colours (green, brown, orange), whereas older children will be able to differentiate between different shades (light green, dark green, light brown, dark brown, etc.).

- Practitioners can support children by talking about the similarities and differences of natural materials.

- You can adapt this by sorting patterns such as natural materials with stripes or spots.

In addition, using scrap and recycled resources will teach children about sustainability and repurposing items, creating an ethos based around caring for the environment and the planet.

Create your own scrap store

Encourage children to reuse scrap materials throughout the provision by adding tin cans to the construction play, egg boxes for junk modelling and bottle tops for counting. This is a great opportunity to talk to young children about reuse and the environment.

As part of our learning about the environment, we have created a scrap store in our setting which is simply shelving units filled with collected resources from conkers to frames, chair legs to milk bottles and buttons to jars. Practitioners, parents and children all donate items to the scrap store which means we have an endless supply of resources to rotate that haven't cost a penny.

TECHNOLOGY

There are lots of ways that children can develop their understanding of technology through loose parts play. When we look at the technology aspect of development, it's about children learning to use switches, remote controls and electronic devices which can all be incorporated quite easily into loose parts play.

One of the most mesmerising loose parts a child will have the opportunity to explore is light. By adding torches and projectors to the continuous provision young children can explore how they can manipulate light. They will explore casting shadows, blocking light and reflecting light off mirrors and windows, all whilst learning how to use technology.

Light boxes, tables and cubes add another element of exploration for lots of loose parts especially those that let the light through such as leaves, transparent plastic counters and fabric. Remote control colour changing cubes are a great way to allow children to explore how remote controls work. Children can also explore how different coloured lights change the colour of different materials and objects.

Changing colours

Technology can bring a whole new perspective to loose parts. This idea will allow children to explore familiar loose parts in a new way whilst also using light as a loose part.

What you need:

- Colour changing cube (alternatively you can create different coloured light by taping coloured transparent film over torch lights)

- Organza fabric squares in different colours

- Transparent film squares in different colours

- Lace doilies

What to do:

- Different coloured lights will change the colour of organza and transparent film squares, e.g. yellow transparent film will appear green when a blue light is shone directly at it. Using the colour changing cube will have the same effect when the organza or transparent film is placed on top.

- Fabric doilies can be placed under the transparent film or organza, when on the light cube, to stop the light in certain areas. Children will notice that these areas (where the doily blocks the light) stay yellow whilst the rest turns blue, leading to lots of discussions about how and why.

- Children can collect items from your continuous provision to further explore their findings and to see which other materials can be manipulated by the light.

Camcorders and cameras can be used alongside loose parts to document non-permanent structures and pieces of art. Children can be a part of the process from capturing the image to uploading it to a computer and printing it out or emailing it to a parent. As more and more settings move towards online learning journals to document each child's learning, we can use this alongside the children by allowing them to take photographs and create voice notes explaining their loose parts play.

Conclusion

Loose parts give children opportunities to explore and learn in line with their thoughts and ideas, often through their experiences in the home and through their relationships with others. We have also seen how open-ended resources and experiences compliment the differences in each child's life, in addition to how technology can be incorporated into play with loose parts.

Expressive art and design is split into two aspects: exploring and using media and materials, and being imaginative. Both of these aspects play a crucial role in loose parts play as exploration and imagination are key to children being given freedom to lead their own learning.

EXPLORING AND USING MEDIA AND MATERIALS

When looking at exploring and using media and materials, this begins as children start to understand the world around them. As they develop, children start to experiment through their sensory experiences and music. Children will also be interested in the marks they can create and will experiment with colours. As children further develop they will begin to move rhythmically and explore sounds made by both their bodies and other objects. They will also begin to use different materials and techniques for a planned purpose.

Babies will explore media and materials using their senses, so providing lots of sensory experiences for young children to engage with is key. There are many types of sensory experiences that incorporate loose parts. As part of technology, we looked at using light as a loose part. This is a great way to stimulate the senses and there are lots of ways children can explore light such as through light up blocks, pebbles, boxes and balls that are suitable for even babies. We can also offer children opportunities to learn through malleable materials by providing tuff trays or bowls filled with new materials to explore and make marks with or in.

Exploring different mediums and materials with babies

There are lots of materials and combinations of materials that children can explore. Babies and younger children will enjoy using their bodies and hands to manipulate materials and to gain an understanding of how they work. As babies often explore through their mouths it's important that everything is non-toxic and that babies are closely observed during this type of play.

Ideas:

- Coloured rice
- Shaving foam
- Sand
- Water
- Ice
- Coloured pasta
- Sand foam (sand and shaving foam)
- Flour and water
- Cornflour and water
- Jelly
- Snow

When children explore sensory and messy play they often explore how they manipulate materials using their bodies. We can do so many different things with our bodies: we can move them in various ways and create numerous noises with them. Children will enjoy listening to different types of music and expressing their ideas through movement. For younger children, we can model movement and dancing. For older children, we can encourage them to think about how the music makes them feel and how they might express that through their movements. Not only can we explore sounds through listening to music and musical instruments, but we can encourage children to think about the noises they can create using their bodies: stamping, clapping, clicking fingers and much more.

What sounds can you make?
. . . .

This activity encourages children to explore sound using their bodies and other materials available within continuous provision. It's also a great activity for developing early phonics skills.

What you need:

- An array of loose parts

What to do:

- Ask the children about different sounds: what does rain sound like? What does thunder sounds like? What does a car sound like?

- Encourage the children to select objects from your continuous provision to recreate the sounds. They might shake some glass beads together or hit two sticks together.

- Further explore the sound. Can the children make the sound with their bodies? Children might stamp their feet or pop their mouths to recreate different sounds.

Another area that's one of the best forms of loose parts play is art. This is because it's individual to each child. It allows freedom and creativity, in addition to lots of opportunities to try out new ways of doing things. Take paint as an example, there are lot of different paints to explore from poster paint to watercolours, acrylic paints to powder paints; all of which create a different effect. That's before we have even begun to look at what happens to each of the paints when we add water to them, mix them together or apply them to different papers. Children will have no problem getting to grips with paint and discovering new ways of using it. It's practitioners that need to understand that the process is necessary.

It's the age-old debate of process versus product that we need to consider. More and more practitioners are beginning to understand that the end product isn't important and that children gain nothing from making the same Christmas card in a conveyer belt style activity where their input is minimal. Instead of emphasising that the end product isn't important, it's time to start thinking about why the process is important and what the process looks like.

LOOKING FOR LEARNING:
FABRIC DYEING

After exploring painting fabrics with the children, I decided to extend this by setting out different types of fabrics on a table alongside powder paints and water.

Observation: As different children accessed the materials it could be clearly seen that each had their own individual approach. One child sprinkled powder paints onto the fabric and then added water using a paintbrush, others simply mixed the powder paint and water together before adding it to the fabric.

As the exploration continued and children shared their ideas, more and more techniques for dyeing the fabric were discovered. This included wetting the fabric then sprinkling powder paints onto it and even using the large bowls of water (that had now changed colour) to dip the whole piece of fabric into. Some children even experimented with how the different colours overlapped when they sprinkled different colours on top of one another.

What are the children learning? This is the perfect example of how practitioners might stunt the process if they take over the experience. As an adult, I know exactly how I would have approached dyeing the fabric but by allowing the children to figure it out for themselves, what they ended up creating was much more effective than what I would have done.

We can see from the above observation that it was the process that took centre stage, not the outcome. However, that doesn't mean that the outcome isn't important for the child; whatever the outcome may be, it's a representation of the process and the learning that took place.

Process art ideas

Instead of setting out specific art activities, set up materials that allow children to explore the process. For example, instead of setting up a stamping activity and showing the children what to do, simply provide the resources and see what they do with them. Here are some resource combinations you could provide:

- Paint, sponges and fabric
- Water, paintbrushes and stones
- Glue, paint and paper
- Clay, water and paintbrushes
- Glue, sand and fabric
- Powder paint, glue and paper
- Paint, water and fabric

BEING IMAGINATIVE

When looking at being imaginative, as with exploring and using media and materials, babies will need to build up their communication skills and understanding of the world before being able to express themselves through pretend play and drawing. As children further develop, they will enjoy singing and making up their own songs, creating and engaging in role play, as well as capturing experiences through art activities such as painting.

Loose parts are great for imaginative play because they have the potential to be anything. A wooden disc can be part of a structure: it can be a cheese slice, it can even be a telephone. Children can imagine anything to be anything if they're given resources that are open to interpretation. This is another area of learning where we can see how beneficial deconstructed role play is. It gives children the ability to be imaginative and create anything they want without adult restrictions placed on their play.

Deconstructed role play has a key role when it comes to allowing children to be imaginative. We have already discussed deconstructed role play and its many benefits (page 34), including how it allows young children to use their imaginations, but we must also remember that a lot of imaginative play happens in the outdoor environment where children are given more space and freedom. Think about what you have outdoors for children to use to extend their role play such as larger loose parts, boxes of fabric and open-ended resources that will spark their curiosity.

LOOKING FOR LEARNING:
THIS IS MY CHRISTMAS TREE

Observation: A group of children were busy building structures with the log slices and various other loose parts. One child used short cardboard tubes to separate his log slices and then began to place glass beads and other small loose parts around the outer edge of each log slice. Once he had finished he proudly exclaimed, 'This is my Christmas tree.'

What are the children learning? As this observation was in July, Christmas was far from my mind and I would never have thought to set up anything Christmas related for the children to explore. This shows how loose parts really do allow children to take control and to follow their own thoughts and ideas, not limiting their imaginations.

Conclusion

When it comes to expressive art and design there is no better way for children to develop than through the use of open-ended materials, loose parts and their imaginations. By providing lots of different loose parts, including paint and clay, and taking on a 'process over product' attitude practitioners need to do little else to ensure young children do what comes naturally to them: exploring, discovering and experimenting.

References

Casey, T. and Robertson, J. (2016), *Loose Parts Play: A toolkit*. Edinburgh: Inspiring Scotland.

Daly, L. and Beloglovsky, M. (2015), *Loose Parts: Inspiring Play in Young Children*. St. Paul: Redleaf Press.

Department for Education (2017), 'Statutory framework for the early years foundation stage: Setting the standards for learning, development and care for children from birth to five', available at: https://www.foundationyears.org.uk/files/2017/03/EYFS_STATUTORY_FRAMEWORK_2017.pdf

Early Education (2012), 'Development Matters in the Early Years Foundation Stage', available at: https://www.foundationyears.org.uk/wp-content/uploads/2012/03/Development-Matters-FINAL-PRINT-AMENDED.pdf

Gibson, J. J. (1986), *The Ecological Approach to Visual Perception*. Abingdon: Taylor & Francis Group.

Monaghan, P. (2018), 'Closing the word gap: What contributes to the variation in children's language development in the early years?'. *National Literacy Trust*, available at: https://medium.com/national-literacy-trust/closing-the-word-gap-812b2b41b413

Moorhouse, P. (2015), 'Woodwork in the early years', available at: https://irresistible-learning.co.uk/wp-content/uploads/2018/01/Woodwork-in-Early-Years-Education.pdf

Nicholson, S. (1972), 'The Theory of Loose Parts: An important principle for design and methodology', *Open University*, 4(2), 5-14.

Piaget, J. (1953), *The Origin of Intelligence in the Child Volume III*. Trans. by M. Cook. Abingdon: Routledge.